[MATTHEW LIVINGSTON]

advisor) before using any of the suggested remedies, techniques, or information in this book.

Upon using the contents and information contained in this book, you agree to hold harmless the Author from and against any damages, costs, and expenses, including any legal fees potentially resulting from the application of any of the information provided by this book. This disclaimer applies to any loss, damages or injury caused by the use and application, whether directly or indirectly, of any advice or information presented, whether for breach of contract, tort, negligence, personal injury, criminal intent, or under any other cause of action.

You agree to accept all risks of using the information presented inside this book.

You agree that by continuing to read this book, where appropriate and/or necessary, you shall consult a professional (including but not limited to your doctor, attorney, or financial advisor or such other advisor as needed) before using any of the suggested remedies, techniques, or information in this book.

Table of Contents

Introduction

If you own any cast-iron cookware then you will know the satisfaction that comes from cooking with them. No matter how many technological advancements come along in terms of cooking surfaces and materials nothing is yet to compare to the classic cast-iron skillet.

Easy to clean, a brilliant non-stick surface, ability to use it in the oven as well as on the stove, near perfect distribution and a bunch of other amazing features make the simple cast iron skillet arguably the best piece of cookware available to you.

Throw in the fact that they are very cheap compared to 'high-tech' pans and that they last for an incredible length of time and it's not hard to see why this classic piece of equipment has survived the test of time.

However, for many people the joy of cooking with cast-iron cookware isn't because of any of the above benefits, it's for the nostalgia factor. This is one of the main reasons I love to cook with my cast-iron skillet, I can still picture a younger me watching my mum cook and I always remember how she seemed to use her cast-iron skillet for everything.

I would watch her make soups, pastas, breads, desserts and everything in between with seeming ease and the apparent need to never use another type of pan. Those are fond times for me to look back on and partially why I decided to write this book.

The other reason I wanted to write it and develop a recipe collection specific to cast-iron skillets is that I think many people under utilize their cast-iron cookware. I wanted to give you a set of recipes that utilize the full functionality of a cast-iron skillet so you can fall back in love with the most awesome piece of kitchenware.

In this book, you're going to learn how to make some of my favorite recipes that are all best cooked in a cast-iron skillet. The features of the pan and the ability to transfer it back and forth between your oven open the doors to some awesomely delicious recipes and in this book you're going to learn the best of the best.

I'm going to show you amazing breakfast, lunch and dinner recipes that are quick to make and taste absolutely brilliant. Plus I've added a free bonus gift onto the book for you, so don't forget to grab it and get delicious dessert recipes. The link is at the front of the book.

So, if you're ready to turn the page and let's get started cooking some delicious meals in your cast-iron skillet.

Chapter 1: Cast Iron Care

When you think of a material such as Iron, the last words that come to mind are: delicate, fragile, or frail. Yet, these things can be said when maintaining cast iron skillets and pans. Now, this doesn't mean you can snap or break a cast iron material with bare hands or in some other barbaric way. I'm referring to the attention to detail and the procedures needed to clean a cast iron utensil.

Cast iron utensils are of a different breed than your average pot or skillet. They are higher in quality and as expected, require more finesse when maintaining. You wouldn't take a Lamborghini to a Ford shop, would you? Then, neither should you put dish soap (or steel wool, or any conventional dish cleaning material) to your cast iron, it's not just "another dish".

But don't let all the talk of delicateness fool you, cast iron utensils definitely are worth the effort and care.

What You'll Need

-Cast Iron Skillet

-Sponge or Stiff Brush

-Paper Towels or Dry Cloth

-Vegetable Oil or Shortening

-(Optional) Kosher Salt

How To Clean

It is best to clean the skillet as soon as you are done using it. If at all possible, while the skillet is still somewhat hot or warm. Leaving the skillet to soak in water or in the sink warrants a high risk of the cast iron rusting. Remember to avoid those things every time you use cast iron.

Apply a sponge soaked in hot water to the areas that need cleaning. You may also use a stiff brush for similar effect. Be cautious to avoid using any kind of dish soap, a dishwashing machine, or steel wool. All of these can result in stripping the cast iron of its seasoning. Which leaves the skillet rust filled.

When you have food residue that doesn't wish to part with the skillet, there are a few crafty ways to get the food off. One of which is to apply Kosher Salt and water to the skillet and scrub it with the sponge or brush mentioned in the previous step. Some people suggest boiling water as a means of easily getting the food residue off. But I do not. Mainly because doing so can be very counterproductive. Boiling water in cast iron can easily, and often does cause cast iron to lose its seasoning. It'll cost you more time to reseason the utensil than it would if you would apply salt and water to it.

The next step in the process is to dry the skillet off. This is best done, using dry towels. If you have time to spare or will be at home for some time, then another way is to dry the skillet using the stove on low heat.

And lastly, making sure the cast iron is back in tip-top condition for future use. Grab a paper towel and some vegetable oil/shortening, and apply a light coat of the substance around the inside of the pot. Some like to use oil on the outside of the pot as well, to keep the look in nice condition. Almost like cleaning a car!

So there you have it. No matter how long you plan on using your cast iron, this process should work every time without a hitch! The key things to remember are the DON'Ts. No dishwashers, dish soaps, steel wools (there are a few that aren't as abrasive as the standard, but better safe than sorry I say), and don't drop cast iron in with the rest of the poor dishes in the sink, waiting for you to finish watching your favorite TV show. Do these things and your cast iron may be able to be passed down to your children as a family heirloom! Some have houses, some have dresses, and some have seasoned cast iron!

Maintenance for Your Cast Iron

Seasoning your cast iron skillet whenever it looks rusted or dull is the maintenance that you will do on a regular basis. Seasoning the skillet is very important and will help keep your skillet its best.

When it comes to washing your skillet, always rinse the skillet immediately after cooking. Run hot water over it, and wipe it clean. For food that is stuck on, use a non-metal brush and scrub with coarse salt. This will help remove the food without wrecking the skillet.

Dry the skillet thoroughly. Leaving a cast iron skillet wet will cause rust to form on the skillet, and this will shorten the life of your pan. If rust does form, use steel wool to remove the rust. Do not use it on other parts of the skillet. Once the rust is removed, go through the seasoning process with the skillet.

Finally, whenever you wash your skillet, spray it with a small amount cooking oil. Then place a paper towel inside the pan to store.

And that is all you need to do to maintain your cast iron skillet.

Chapter 2: Health Benefits of Cast Iron

Although you wouldn't think of a skillet as something with health benefits, there are a number of health benefits that you can get by cooking with a cast iron skillet. These health benefits are:

1. You generally use less oil.

Because of how you season a cast iron skillet, you will find that your recipes do not require as much oil as they used to. This means less fat and food that has more flavor than grease. Both will help with your health. For one, you will enjoy the taste of your food and be less inclined to eat out and the other means that your meals are leaner.

2. You are exposed to fewer chemicals.

Cast iron is a natural choice when it comes to cooking. Most skillets that are not cast iron have a spray coating on them to make them non-stick. This coating contains several chemicals including perfluorocarbons, which are released into the air and into your food during cooking.

These chemicals are linked to liver damage, developmental problems in children and cancer.

Cast iron, as long has it has not been coated, is free from those chemicals and does not leave any chemicals in your food.

3. You will have an iron boost.

Finally, cast iron offers an increase of iron in your food, a huge benefit. Many people, especially women, have an iron deficiency. Cooking with cast iron helps boost iron by as much as 20% of your daily iron intake.

Chapter 3: Tips for Cooking with Cast Iron

The final thing that I want to touch on before we get into the recipes is to offer a few helpful tips that will make cooking with cast iron much easier. These are:

1. Always Preheat

Make sure that you always preheat your cast iron skillet. It can take a bit of time for the cast iron to heat up, so putting the food in too soon can cause your food to be undercooked or to take longer to cook. Preheating it will ensure that your food is being cooked on the best temperature every time.

2. Cook on Medium Temperatures

Although it does take time for cast iron to heat up, once it does, it maintains its heat for long periods. Cooking on high temperatures will result in your food burning, so always cook on medium temperatures -- medium-low through medium-high.

3. Don't Be Afraid to Make it Versatile

If there is a tool that is truly versatile it's the cast iron skillet. You can use it as a frying pan, a deep fryer, and even as a baking dish. One of the best things is that you can easily move your cast iron skillet from stove top to oven without having to do anything to it.

Experiment with your cast iron, and you will find it is really enjoyable to use. In fact, many of the recipes in this book will have you using your cast iron skillet as more than just a frying pan.

4. Reduce Cooking Times

Whenever you are using a recipe that is not designed for the cast iron skillet, make sure that you reduce cooking times a bit. Remember that the cast iron skillet maintains its heat for quite a while so you can cook the dish almost to completion, turn down the temperature or turn off the stove, and let the pan do the rest of the cooking.

Note: Always watch your food if you are leaving it in the cast iron skillet for serving since the food can burn if the pan is still hot.

5. Watch that Heat

Finally, watch the temperature of the pan. Since the handles are not covered, they will get as hot as the pan itself. It's a good idea to always wear oven mitts when handling your cast iron skillet to prevent burns.

So now that you know the tips; grab your cast iron skillets and let's get started on the recipes!

Chapter 4: Breakfast Recipes

Steak and Eggs Benedict

Servings: 4

Preparation time: 10 minutes

Cooking time: 20 to 40 minutes

Ingredients:

- 8 egg yolks

- 1 tablespoon of black pepper

- 1 tablespoon of salt

- 1 16 ounces Strip Steak

- 3 tablespoons of vegetable oil

- 8 eggs

- 1 French Baguette

- 2 tablespoons of butter

- 1 cup of butter, unsalted

- 4 tablespoons of lemon juice

- 1/4 teaspoon of salt

- 1/4 teaspoon of white pepper

- Dash of Hot Pepper

Preparation:

1. Place a cast iron skillet on the stove, and set to medium-high.

2. Add the oil, and heat until sizzling.

3. While the oil is heating, combine the black pepper and tablespoon of salt. Mix thoroughly.

4. Rub the salt mixture onto the steak.

5. Place the steak into the oil, and cook until the steak is medium rare. The best way to do this is to cook the steak for about 3 to 5 minutes on each side. Make sure you only turn the steak once to get the best flavoring.

6. Remove the steak from the heat, and allow to cool slightly before slicing it into 1/2" slices.

7. While the steak is cooling, slice the baguette into 1/2" slices. Toast each piece of baguette. Set to the side.

8. Separate the egg yolks from the egg whites. You can keep the egg whites for a different recipe or throw them away.

9. In a blender, combine the egg yolks and lemon juice.

10. Add the hot sauce, and blend the mixture for about 20 seconds or until it is well blended. Make sure you use the lowest setting as you do not want to make the eggs frothy.

11. Add in the cup of butter, and blend for 2 to 3 minutes or until the butter is fully mixed, and you have a thin mixture.

12. Blend in the white pepper and 1/4 teaspoon of salt. Set aside this mixture as it is a Hollandaise sauce.

13. In a fresh cast iron skillet (the best size is a 10"), add the 2 tablespoons of butter, and place the skillet on the stove set to medium heat.

14. Once the butter is melted, carefully crack the eggs into the pan. Don't overcrowd the eggs. You may have to do the eggs in batches.

15. Cook until the eggs are the desired consistency. With this dish, the yolks should be glossy and the whites should be set.

16. Remove the eggs from the heat.

17. Place a few slices of steak onto each baguette toast.

18. Add a fried egg to the top of the steak. There should only be one egg per baguette toast.

19. Spoon on the Hollandaise sauce, which is the egg yolk and lemon juice mixture that you made in the blender.

20. Serve warm.

Breakfast Scramble

Servings: 6

Preparation time: 5 minutes

Cooking time: 10 minutes

Ingredients:

- 12 eggs

- 1 red onion

- 1 jalapeno

- 2 tablespoons of chives, diced

- 2 tablespoons of butter, unsalted

- 1/4 teaspoon of salt

- 1/4 teaspoon of black pepper

- 1/2 cup of goat cheese (1/2 cup of feta cheese or cheddar cheese as a substitute for goat cheese)

Preparation:

1. Place a large, 12" cast iron skillet on the stove, and set the heat to medium.

2. Wash, peel, and dice the red onion.

3. Wash and cut the jalapeno into circles. Keep the seeds with the cut pepper.

4. Add the butter to the skillet and melt.

5. Pour in the onion and jalapeno, and sauté for about 5 to 7 minutes or until the peppers and onions are soft.

6. In a separate bowl, whisk together the eggs.

7. Whisk in the salt and pepper.

8. Pour the eggs into the skillet and cook, stirring frequently, until you have the desired consistency. Usually takes about 3 to 5 minutes.

9. While the eggs are cooking, crumble the goat cheese. If you are using cheddar cheese, shred it, or crumble the feta cheese.

10. Wash and dice the fresh chives.

11. Remove the eggs from the stove and fold in the cheese and chives.

12. Serve warm.

Farm House Breakfast

Servings: 4

Preparation time: 20 minutes

Cooking time: 30 minutes

Ingredients:

- 3 cups of red skinned potatoes

- 8 eggs

- 1/4 cup of parsley leaves, chopped and fresh

- 1/4 teaspoon of black pepper

- 3 tablespoons of butter

- 1 teaspoon of salt

- 2 garlic cloves

- 1 cup of farmhouse cheddar, shredded

Preparation:

1. Preheat the oven to 400°F.

2. Wash the potatoes, but do not peel them.

3. Chop the potatoes into small hash browns, usually smaller than a half inch.

4. Wash and chop the parsley leaves.

5. Place a 10" to 12" cast iron skillet onto the stove, and set the heat to medium.

6. Add the butter, and allow the butter to melt completely.

7. Place the potatoes into the butter, and sauté for about 15 minutes or until the potatoes are tender and have started to brown.

8. Mince the garlic, and stir into the potatoes, cook for an additional minute.

9. Fold in the salt and pepper.

10. Add the parsley, cook for another minute.

11. Remove the cast iron pan from the stove.

12. Using the back of a wooden spoon, create an indent into the potato. Make 4 indents; one for two eggs.

13. Carefully break two eggs into each indentation.

14. Place in the oven, and bake until the egg whites are cooked. This usually takes about 10 minutes.

15. Once the eggs have the consistency you want, shred the farmhouse cheese.

16. Remove the cast iron skillet from the oven and sprinkle the cheese over the eggs.

17. Return to the oven, and bake for 1 to 2 minutes or until the cheese has melted.

18. Remove from the oven and serve warm.

Berry Pancakes

Servings: 4

Preparation time: 10 minutes

Cooking time: 20 minutes

Ingredients:

- 1 cup of flour, all purpose

- 1/4 cup of white sugar

- 1 cup of milk

- 2 tablespoons of butter, unsalted

- 4 eggs

- 1/4 teaspoon of salt

- 1/2 teaspoon of lemon zest

- 1/2 cup of blueberries

- 1/2 cup of raspberries

Preparation:

1. Preheat the oven to 400°F.

2. Sift the flour into a bowl.

3. Zest the lemon, and add to the flour.

4. Add the salt.

5. In a separate bowl, whisk together the eggs and milk.

6. Slowly add the egg mixture to the flour mixture. Mix until the ingredients are well blended and you have a smooth batter.

7. Wash and stem the blueberries. Place in a separate bowl.

8. Wash and cut the raspberries in half. Place the raspberries in the same bowl as the blueberries, and toss the fruit together.

9. Place a cast iron skillet onto the stove, and set the heat to high. Make sure that you use a 12" skillet.

10. When the skillet is hot, add the butter and allow it to melt.

11. Once the butter is melted, pour the batter into the hot skillet. Turn the skillet slightly to make sure the batter covers the entire pan.

12. Add the berry mixture to the top of the batter. You should scatter the berries so they are all over the entire batter. Don't worry if the berries sink into the batter.

13. Remove from the stove, and place the cast iron skillet into the oven.

14. Bake for 20 minutes or until the pastry is baked completely through and is puffed.

15. Remove from the oven, serve warm with syrup, icing sugar, or whipped cream.

Servings: 6

Preparation time: 10 minutes

Cooking time: 35 minutes

Ingredients:

- 6 cups of frozen hash browns

- 6 eggs

- 6 slices of bacon

- 1 green pepper

- 1/2 cup of onion, chopped

- 1/2 cup of cheddar cheese, shredded

- 1/4 teaspoon of pepper

- 1 teaspoon of salt

Preparation:

1. Place a 10" cast iron skillet onto the stove and set the temperature to medium.

2. Chop the bacon, and place it into the skillet.

3. Cook the bacon until it is crispy, usually about 5 to 10 minutes.

4. Drain the bacon, but reserve 2 tablespoons of the bacon grease. You can dispose of the rest.

5. Set aside the bacon, and return the cast iron skillet to the stove without washing it or getting a clean one. You want the flavor of the bacon that will still be in the pan.

6. Add the bacon grease.

7. Wash and seed the green pepper. Chop it.

8. Wash, peel, and chop the onion.

9. Pour the potatoes into the skillet.

10. Add in the green pepper and onion. Stir until the vegetables are well blended.

11. Season with the salt and pepper, and cook for about 2 minutes.

12. Stir the ingredients, and then cover the cast iron skillet with a lid.

13. Cook the vegetables until the hash browns are golden brown, usually about 15 minutes. Make sure that you stir the hash browns every few minutes to prevent

burning, but don't over stir them or you will turn the mixture to mush.

14. Once the hash browns are tender, using the back of a wooden spoon, create an indent into the potato. Make 4 indents; one for two eggs.

15. Carefully break an egg into each indentation.

16. Cover the cast iron skillet with the lid again and continue to cook on medium heat until the eggs have the proper consistency, usually about 8 to 10 minutes.

17. Shred the cheese, and toss it with the bacon.

18. When the eggs are cooked to the desired consistency, remove the cast iron skillet from the stove.

19. Sprinkle the dish with cheese and bacon, cover for a minute to allow the cheese to melt slightly, then serve warm.

Spicy Potato Hash Browns

Servings: 4

Preparation time: 25 minutes

Cooking time: 35 minutes

Ingredients:

- 5 baking potatoes

- 1/4 teaspoon of black pepper

- 1/4 teaspoon of onion powder

- 1/2 teaspoon of salt

- 1/4 teaspoon of thyme, dried

- 1 teaspoon of fresh thyme

- 1/4 cup of vegetable oil

- 1/4 teaspoon of oregano

- 1/2 teaspoon of garlic powder

- 2 teaspoon of minced garlic

- 1 cup of yellow onion, diced

- 3 tablespoons of butter

- 1/4 teaspoon of cayenne pepper

Preparation:

1. Wash the potatoes, and place them in a pot.

2. Fill with water, and place on the stove set to high.

3. Bring to a boil, and cook the potatoes until they are half cooked, usually about 15 minutes after the water boils.

4. Drain the water, and allow the potatoes to cool.

5. Remove the skins from the potatoes while they are still warm.

6. Chop the potatoes into 1/2" hash browns.

7. Wash, peel, and dice the yellow onions.

8. Mince the fresh garlic

9. Place the 12" cast iron skillet onto the stove and set the temperature to high.

10. Pour in the oil.

11. Add the butter, and heat thoroughly. Add the onions.

12. Sauté the onions until they begin to tender, usually about 3 to 5 minutes.

13. Add the minced garlic to the onions, stirring for about a minute or until the smell of garlic grows strong.

14. Fold in the potatoes, and stir until the potatoes are mixed well with the onions.

15. Chop the fresh thyme, and add it to the potatoes along with the salt and pepper.

16. Sprinkle on the dried thyme, oregano, onion powder, garlic powder, and cayenne pepper. Do not stir in the ingredients. Simply shake the pan to keep the potatoes from burning.

17. Allow the ingredients to cook until the bottom of the potatoes is golden brown, usually about 4 to 6 minutes.

18. Using a spatula, turn the potatoes.

19. Cook on the other side until the potatoes are golden brown throughout, usually an additional 4 minutes.

20. Remove from heat and serve warm.

Servings: 6

Preparation time: 10 minutes

Cooking time: 30 minutes

Ingredients:

- 3 cups of potatoes

- 2 tablespoons of vegetable oil

- 1 onion

- 1 red bell pepper

- 6 eggs

- 1 garlic clove

- 1 tablespoon of butter

- 1/4 teaspoon of pepper

Preparation:

1. Preheat the oven to 350°F.

2. Wash and peel the potatoes.

3. Shred the potatoes, and place in a bowl of cold water so the potatoes are completely covered. Let them sit for 5 minutes.

4. While the potatoes are sitting, place a cast iron skillet onto the stove. The best size to use for this meal is a 10" pan.

5. Add the butter, and set the heat to medium.

6. Pour in the oil. Heat the oil and butter.

7. Wash and seed the bell pepper. Dice it into small portions.

8. Wash, peel, and chop the onion.

9. Place both vegetables into the hot pan, and sauté until the onions are tender, usually 3 to 5 minutes.

10. When the onions are cooked, mince the garlic, and add to the onion mixture. Sauté for a minute.

11. Remove the potatoes from the water, and drain them on a paper towel. Place the shredded potatoes into the pan, and mix until the onion mixture is well blended.

12. Continue to grill until the potatoes are golden brown and tender, usually about 10 minutes.

13.Once the potatoes are tender, remove from the heat.

14.Using the back of a wooden spoon, create an indentation in the potato. Make 6 indents; one for each egg.

15.Carefully break an egg into each indentation.

16.Sprinkle the eggs with pepper.

17.Place the cast iron skillet into the oven, and bake the dish for 12 to 14 minutes or until the eggs are the desired consistency.

18.Remove from the oven and serve warm.

Servings: 4

Preparation time: 10 minutes

Cooking time: 20 minutes

Ingredients:

- 3 tomatoes

- 1/2 cup of onion, chopped

- 4 eggs

- 2 tablespoons of olive oil

- 1/2 teaspoon of salt

- 4 teaspoons of fresh oregano

- 4 teaspoons of fresh chives

- 4 teaspoons of fresh basil

- 1/2 teaspoon of pepper

- 1/2 cup of mozzarella cheese

Preparation:

1. Wash the tomatoes, and chop into bite-sized pieces.

2. Wash, peel, and chop the onion.

3. Place a 10" cast iron skillet onto the stove, and set to medium heat.

4. Pour in the oil and heat.

5. Once the oil is hot, place in the chopped onion.

6. Sauté the onion until it is tender and almost translucent; between 3 to 5 minutes.

7. Fold in the tomatoes and season with the salt and pepper.

8. Cook the vegetables for about 5 minutes, or until the tomatoes are soft. Stir frequently while cooking.

9. Once the tomatoes are soft, using a wooden spoon, make an indentation in the tomato mixture.

10. Repeat until you have four wells or indentations in the tomatoes.

11. Carefully crack an egg into each well.

12. Place a lid on the cast iron skillet, and continue to cook until the whites are firm and the yolks are still soft. This can take anywhere from 5 to 10 minutes.

13. Shred the mozzarella cheese

14. Once the eggs are the desired consistency, sprinkle the dish with the shredded cheese.

15. Return the lid to the skillet, and cook for an additional minute.

16. Wash and chop the oregano, basil, and chives. Toss together.

17. Remove from heat, and sprinkle the herbs on top.

18. Serve on its own or with toast.

Chapter 5: Lunch

Mole Chile and Cornbread

Serves: 6

Preparation time: 15 minutes

Cooking time: 45 minutes

Ingredients:

- 1 pound ground beef

- 4 cloves garlic, crushed and minced

- 2 cups black beans (canned or precooked)

- 1 cup kidney beans (canned or precooked)

- 1 15 ounces can fire roasted tomatoes

- 2 cups fresh corn kernels

- 4 cups beef stock

- 2 tablespoons tomato paste

- 2 tablespoons unsweetened cocoa powder

- ¼ cup smoked paprika

- 1 tablespoon ancho chili powder

- 1 teaspoon cinnamon

- 1 teaspoon salt

- 1 teaspoon black pepper

- 1 cup cornmeal mix

- 1 egg, beaten

- ¼ cup of vegetable oil

- ¾ cup whole milk

- 1 cup cheddar cheese, shredded

- Scallions for garnish

Preparation:

1. Preheat the oven to 425°F/218°C.
2. Prepare a 12-inch deep cast iron skillet and add the ground beef and garlic. Cook over medium heat for 5-7 minutes, or until browned. Drain off any residual grease from the meat.
3. Add the black beans, kidney beans, fire roasted tomatoes, and corn. Stir to mix.
4. Gently push the ingredients to the outside perimeter of the skillet. To the center add the

beef stock, tomato paste, cocoa powder, smoked paprika, ancho chili powder, and cinnamon.

5. Stir the center to mix the seasonings together and then begin to incorporate the rest of the ingredients, eventually mixing everything together throughout the entire skillet. Season with salt and black pepper as desired.

6. Reduce heat to low and let simmer while the cornbread topping is prepared.

7. In a bowl, combine the cornmeal mix, egg, vegetable oil, whole milk, and cheddar cheese. Pour the mixture over the chili and spread, starting in the center and spreading out toward the edges of the pan.

8. Place in the oven and bake for 25-30 minutes, or until the top is golden brown.

9. Garnish with scallions before serving.

Shrimp Piccata

Serves: 4

Preparation time: 10 minutes

Cooking time: 15 minutes

Ingredients:

- 1 pound raw shrimp, cleaned and deveined

- 2 tablespoons butter

- 3 cloves garlic, crushed and minced

- ¼ cup shallots, sliced

- ¼ cup capers

- ¼ cup lemon juice

- 1 cup dry white wine

- 1 ½ cups chicken stock

- 1 teaspoon salt

- 1 teaspoon black pepper

- ½ pound angel hair pasta

- Fresh parsley for garnish

Preparation:

1. Prepare a 10- or 12-inch cast iron skillet and melt the butter over medium heat.
2. Add the garlic and shallots. Cook for 1-2 minutes.
3. Add the shrimp, gently tossing while cooking, for 2 minutes.
4. Add the capers, lemon juice, and white wine to the skillet. Let the wine reduce for 1-2 minutes.
5. Add the chicken stock, salt, and black pepper. Stir well. Increase heat to medium-high and bring to a low boil.
6. Add the angel hair pasta, reduce heat back down to medium and cook for 7-10 minutes, or until pasta is al dente.
7. Serve garnished with fresh parsley.

Serves: 4

Preparation time: 10 minutes

Cooking time: 35 minutes

Ingredients:

- 4 pork chops, bone-in, about 8 ounces. each, ¾ to 1-inch thick

- 2 tablespoons olive oil

- 4 cups small red potatoes, halved

- 4 cups green beans, washed and trimmed

- 1 tablespoon fresh dill, chopped

- ½ cup fresh parsley, chopped

- 4 cloves garlic, crushed and minced

- 1 teaspoon paprika

- 1 teaspoon salt

- 1 teaspoon black pepper

Preparation:

1. Preheat oven to 400°F/204°C.

2. Prepare a 12-inch cast iron skillet and brush with olive oil. Place the pork chops in the pan.

3. In a bowl, combine the potatoes and green beans. Drizzle with remaining olive oil and toss to coat. Add the vegetables to the pan with the pork chops.

4. Season with dill, parsley, garlic, paprika, salt, and black pepper. Place the skillet in the oven and bake for 30-35 minutes, or until potatoes are tender and pork chops are cooked through.

Korean Spiced Beef and Jasmine Rice

Serves: 4

Preparation time: 10 minutes

Cooking time: 20 minutes

Ingredients:

- 2 tablespoons vegetable oil

- 1 pound beef steak, cut into thin strips

- ¼ cup of soy sauce

- 2 tablespoons brown sugar

- 1 tablespoon honey

- 1 tablespoon sesame seeds

- 2 teaspoons sesame oil

- 2 teaspoons garlic paste

- 2 cloves garlic, crushed and minced

- 1 cup yellow onion, sliced

- 1 cup savoy cabbage, shredded

- 2 cups broccoli florets

- 1 cup carrots, sliced thin

- 4 cups jasmine rice, cooked

- Scallions, sliced for garnish

Preparation:

1. Prepare a 10- or 12-inch cast iron skillet and add the vegetable oil over medium-high heat. Add the steak and sauté for 2-3 minutes, or until browned. Push meat to the outer edges of the skillet.

2. To the center of the skillet add the soy sauce, brown sugar, honey, sesame seeds, sesame oil, and garlic paste. Stir until fragrant, approximately 1 minute.

3. Add the garlic and onion. Sauté for 2 minutes.

4. Add the savoy cabbage, broccoli, and carrots. Sauté for 3 minutes before introducing the meat back into the center of the pan.

5. Stir in the jasmine rice right before serving.

6. Garnish with fresh scallions.

Tri-Colored Stuffed Pepper Casserole

Serves: 4

Preparation time: 10 minutes

Cooking time: 30 minutes

Ingredients:

- 1 pound ground beef

- 2 tablespoons olive oil

- 3 cloves garlic, crushed and minced

- 1 cup red bell pepper, diced

- 1 cup yellow bell pepper, diced

- 1 cup green bell pepper, diced

- ½ cup red onion, diced

- ¼ cup fresh basil, chopped

- ¼ cup parsley, chopped

- 1 15 ounces can crushed tomatoes, with liquid

- 1 cup tomato sauce

- 2 cups beef stock

- 1 tablespoon Worcestershire sauce

- 1 cup uncooked rice

- 1 teaspoon salt

- 1 teaspoon black pepper

- 1 cup provolone cheese, shredded

- ½ cup parmesan cheese, freshly grated

Preparation:

1. Prepare a 10- or 12-inch cast iron skillet and add the olive oil over medium heat.

2. Cook the ground beef until browned, and drain any fat.

3. Add the garlic, red bell pepper, yellow bell pepper, green bell pepper, and red onion. Sauté for 3-5 minutes.

4. Season with basil and parsley. Add the tomato sauce, beef stock, and Worcestershire sauce. Stir, increase heat to medium-high and bring to a boil.

5. Add the rice, salt, and black pepper. Stir, reduce heat and cover. Simmer for 15-20 minutes, or until rice is tender.

6. Sprinkle the cheese over the rice, cover and cook an additional 5 minutes, or until cheese is melted.

Serves: 6

Preparation time: 10 minutes

Cooking time: 45 minutes

Ingredients:

- 2-3 pounds pork tenderloin roast

- ¼ cup olive oil, divided

- 1 cup sweet yellow onions, sliced

- 3 cloves garlic, crushed and minced

- 1 teaspoon crushed red pepper flakes

- 1 teaspoon paprika

- 1 teaspoon thyme

- 1 cup apple cider

- 3 cups red baking apples, cut into wedges

- 3 cups sweet potatoes, cubed

- ½ teaspoon nutmeg

- ½ teaspoon coriander

- 1 teaspoon salt

- 1 teaspoon black pepper

Preparation:

1. Preheat oven to 425°F/218°C.
2. Prepare a 12-inch cast iron skillet and 2 tablespoons of the olive oil. Heat over medium.
3. Add the onion and garlic. Sauté for 2-3 minutes.
4. Season the tenderloin with crushed red pepper flakes, paprika, and thyme. Place the tenderloin in the skillet and brown evenly on all sides, approximately 2-3 minutes per side. Pour in the apple cider and reduce heat to simmer.
5. Meanwhile, combine the baking apples and sweet potatoes in a bowl. Drizzle with the remaining olive oil and season with nutmeg, coriander, salt, and black pepper. Toss to coat.
6. Add the vegetables to the skillet with the pork. Remove the skillet from the heat and place in the oven. Bake for 30-35 minutes, or until internal temperature measures 160°F/71°C.
7. Let rest 10 minutes before serving.

Smokey Bacon and Crab Chowder

Serves: 4-6

Preparation time: 10 minutes

Cooking time: 30 minutes

Ingredients:

- ½ pound bacon, diced

- 1 cup sweet yellow onion, diced

- 1 cup celery, diced

- 1 cup carrots, diced

- 1 tablespoon fresh thyme

- 1 teaspoon salt

- 1 teaspoon black pepper

- ½ cup dry white wine

- 8 cups red potatoes, cubed

- 2 cups whole milk

- 2 cups fish stock

- 1 cup heavy cream

- 1 cup clam juice

- 1 pound crab meat

- Fresh scallions for garnish

Preparation:

1. Prepare a 12-inch skillet and cook the bacon over medium heat until lightly crisp, approximately 5 minutes.
2. Add yellow onion, celery, and carrots. Season with thyme, salt, and black pepper. Sauté for 3-4 minutes. Add the white wine and cook 1-2 minutes more.
3. Add the potatoes, milk, fish stock, heavy cream, and crab juice. Stir well. Increase heat to medium-high and cook, stirring frequently until potatoes are tender, approximately 10 minutes.
4. Transfer half of the mixture to a blender and blend until smooth. Reincorporate the blended mixture back into the skillet.
5. Add the crab meat and cook until heated through approximately 7-10 minutes.
6. Garnish with fresh scallions.

Lemony Wild Mushroom and Broccoli Pasta

Serves: 4

Preparation time: 10 minutes

Cooking time: 15 minutes

Ingredients:

- 2 cups broccoli florets

- 2 tablespoons olive oil, divided

- 2 cloves garlic, crushed and minced

- 3 cups vegetable stock or water

- 1 pound linguine noodles

- 4 cups wild mushrooms, thinly sliced

- 2 tablespoons lemon juice

- 1 tablespoon lemon zest

- 2 teaspoons fresh thyme

- 1 tablespoon fresh chives

- 1 teaspoon salt

- 1 teaspoon black pepper

- Freshly grated asiago cheese for garnish

Preparation:

1. In a bowl combine the wild mushrooms, 1 tablespoon of olive oil, lemon juice, lemon zest, thyme, chives, salt, and black pepper. Toss to mix.

2. Prepare a 10- or 12-inch cast iron skillet and heat 1 tablespoon of olive oil over medium heat. Add the broccoli florets and sauté until bright green and slightly tender. Transfer to the bowl with the mushrooms and set aside.

3. Add the vegetable stock or water to the skillet and heat over medium-high until lightly boiling. Add the linguine noodles and cook for approximately 7-10 minutes, or until al dente. Drain excess liquid.

4. Transfer the broccoli and mushroom mixture to the pan with the linguine. Toss, while heating over medium-low heat until all ingredients are warmed through and nicely blended.

5. Toss with fresh asiago cheese before serving.

Sweet Potato Burrito Skillet

Serves: 4

Preparation time: 10 minutes

Cooking time: 30 minutes

Ingredients:

- 2 ½ cups sweet potatoes, cubed

- ¼ cup olive oil, divided

- 1 cup yellow onion, diced

- 3 cloves garlic, crushed and minced

- 1 cup red bell peppers, chopped

- 2 cups tomatoes, diced

- 1 cup of rice

- 1 15-ounce can black beans, drained

- 1 ½ cup fresh corn kernels

- 1 teaspoon chili powder

- 1 teaspoon cumin

- 1 teaspoon paprika

- 1 teaspoon salt

- 1 teaspoon black pepper

- ¼ cup fresh cilantro, chopped

- 2 ½ cups vegetable broth

- 1 cup Mexican queso cheese

- 1 cup cheddar cheese

- Sour cream for garnish

Preparation:

1. Prepare a 10- or 12-inch cast iron skillet and heat 2 tablespoons of olive oil over medium heat. Add the sweet potatoes and cook, while stirring, for approximately 7-8 minutes.

2. Add the onion, garlic, and red bell pepper, along with an additional 2 tablespoons of olive oil, if needed. Cook for 5 minutes more.

3. Add the tomatoes, rice, black beans, and corn kernels. Toss to mix and season with chili powder, cumin, paprika, salt, black pepper, and cilantro.

4. Add the vegetable broth and increase heat until broth boils. Reduce heat and allow to simmer for 15 minutes, or until rice is tender.

5. Stir in queso and Mexican cheeses and let melt before serving.

6. Garnish with sour cream.

White Wine Braised Salmon and Baked Potatoes

Serves: 4

Preparation time: 10 minutes

Cooking time: 25 minutes

Ingredients:

- 1 pound salmon fillets

- 1 tablespoon olive oil

- 2 cloves garlic, crushed and minced

- 1 tablespoon fresh dill

- 1 tablespoon fresh chives

- 1 teaspoon lemon zest

- ½ cup dry white wine

- 3 cups green beans, washed and trimmed

- 4 cups yellow potatoes, sliced thin

- 2 teaspoons fresh rosemary

- 1 teaspoon salt

- 1 teaspoon black pepper

Preparation:

1. Preheat oven to 425°F/218°C.

2. Prepare a 10-inch cast iron skillet and heat the olive oil over medium heat. Add the garlic and sauté 1 minute.

3. Add the salmon and season with dill, chives, and lemon zest. Add the white wine to the skillet and cook for two minutes.

4. Add the green beans to the pan. Then layer the potato slices evenly over the salmon and green beans. Season the potatoes with rosemary, salt, and black pepper.

5. Place the skillet in the oven and bake for 15-20 minutes, or until salmon is flaky and pink.

Chapter 6: Dinner

Zesty Eggplant Parmesan

Serves: 4

Preparation time: 10 minutes

Cooking time: 30 minutes

Ingredients:

- ¼ cup of vegetable oil

- 1 medium-sized eggplant, sliced approximately ¼ inch thick

- 2 eggs, beaten

- 1 cup seasoned bread crumbs

- 1 clove garlic, crushed and minced

- 1 cup parmesan cheese, freshly grated, divided

- 2 ½ cups prepared marinara sauce (homemade or jarred)

- 1 tablespoon fresh oregano

- ¼ cup fresh basil, chopped (additional for garnish, if desired)

- 1 teaspoon salt

- 1 teaspoon black pepper

- 1 cup fresh mozzarella cheese, sliced

- 6 cups dark salad greens, for serving.

Preparation:

1. Preheat oven to 350°F/177°C.
2. Place the beaten eggs in one bowl, and in another bowl combine the seasoned bread crumbs, garlic, and ½ cup parmesan cheese.
3. Prepare a 12-inch cast iron skillet and heat the vegetable oil over medium-high heat.
4. Coat each eggplant slice with the beaten egg and then dredge through the breadcrumb mixture.
5. Place the eggplant slices in the pan and cook 2 minutes per side, or until browned. Reserve cooked pieces of eggplant on a side plate as you work through the eggplant in batches.
6. Turn off the heat and layer all pieces of eggplant in the bottom of the skillet. Top with marinara sauce and season with oregano, basil, salt, and black pepper.
7. Top the eggplant with mozzarella cheese and remaining ½ cup parmesan cheese.

8. Place in the oven and bake for 20 minutes or until cheese is golden brown.

9. Serve with fresh dark salad greens.

Serves: 4

Preparation time: 10 minutes

Cooking time: 30 minutes

Ingredients:

- 1 tablespoon olive oil

- 1 cup red onion, diced

- ½ cup red bell pepper

- 4 cloves garlic, crushed and minced

- 1 pound ground beef, crumbled

- ½ cup fresh basil, chopped

- 1 tablespoon fresh oregano, chopped

- 1 teaspoon salt

- 1 teaspoon black pepper

- 4 cups fire roasted canned tomatoes, with liquid

- 10 lasagna noodles, broken into 2-3 inch pieces

- 1 cup fresh mozzarella cheese, shredded

- 1 cup ricotta cheese

- ½ cup parmesan cheese

Preparation:

1. Preheat broiler.

2. Prepare a 12-inch cast iron skillet and heat the olive oil over medium heat.

3. Add the ground beef and cook until browned, approximately 7 minutes. Drain any fat.

4. Add the red onion, bell pepper, and garlic. Cook while stirring until onion and pepper are slightly tender, approximately 3 minutes.

5. Season with basil, oregano, salt, and black pepper. Add in the tomatoes and increase heat to medium-high. Bring to a low boil, add the lasagna noodles, stir and reduce heat to a simmer. Cook for 10 minutes.

6. In a bowl, combine the mozzarella cheese, ricotta cheese, and parmesan cheese. Mix well.

7. Place spoonfuls of the cheese mixture around the skillet.

8. Place the skillet under the broiler for 5-7 minutes, or until cheese is lightly browned.

9. Let cool slightly before serving.

Creamy Basil Flank Steak

Serves: 4

Preparation time: 10 minutes

Cooking time: 30 minutes

Ingredients:

- 2 pounds flank steak, pounded to even thickness

- 1 tablespoon vegetable oil

- 3 cloves garlic, crushed and minced

- 1 teaspoon Worcestershire sauce

- 1 teaspoon salt

- 1 teaspoon black pepper

- 4 cups green beans, washed and trimmed

- ½ cup beef broth

- 1 teaspoon cornstarch

- 2 teaspoons ground black peppercorns

- ¼ cup fresh basil, chopped

- 1 tablespoon chives, chopped

- ½ teaspoon salt

- ½ cup cream cheese softened

Preparation:

1. Prepare a 12-inch cast iron skillet and heat the vegetable oil over medium-high heat.

2. Place the steak in the pan and season with garlic, Worcestershire sauce, salt, and black pepper. Sear on both sides until browned, approximately 10 minutes per side. Remove the steak from the pan and set aside to rest.

3. Meanwhile, add the green beans to the pan and sauté in the meat juices just until color brightens approximately 3-4 minutes. Remove and set aside with the steak.

4. In a small bowl combine the beef broth and cornstarch. Whisk until smooth and add to the hot skillet.

5. Season with black peppercorns, basil, chives, and salt. Mix well.

6. Add the cream cheese and whisk in the pan until the cheese has broken up and blended smoothly with the broth. Cook for 1-2 minutes.

7. Serve the warm basil sauce over the steak with the
   green beans on the side.

Chorizo Tamale Pie

Serves: 4-6

Preparation time: 15 minutes

Cooking time: 30 minutes

Ingredients:

- 1 pound chorizo sausage, crumbled

- 1 cup red onion, diced

- 4 cloves garlic, crushed and minced

- ½ cup poblano pepper, diced

- ½ cup red bell pepper, diced

- 1 tablespoon ancho chili powder

- 2 teaspoons cumin

- 1 teaspoon coriander

- ¼ cup fresh cilantro, chopped

- 1 ½ cup fresh corn kernels

- 1 15 ounces can kidney beans, drained

- 1 28 ounces can tomatoes, crushed with liquid

- 1 cup vegetable or chicken stock

- ½ cup queso cheese, crumbled

- ½ cup cheddar cheese, shredded

- ½ cup butter, melted

- 1 cup cornmeal

- 1 cup flour

- 2 teaspoons baking powder

- 2 eggs, beaten

- 1 tablespoon orange juice

- 2 tablespoons honey

- ¼ cup buttermilk

- 1 cup sour cream

- ½ teaspoon salt

Preparation:

1. Preheat oven to 425°F/218°C.

2. Prepare a 12-inch cast iron skillet and add the chorizo
   over medium heat. Cook for 5 minutes.

3. Add the onion, garlic, poblano pepper, and red bell pepper. Cook, stirring frequently for 4-5 minutes. Season with ancho chili powder, cumin, coriander, and fresh cilantro. Stir well.

4. Add the corn kernels, kidney beans, tomatoes with liquid and vegetable or chicken stock. Increase heat to medium-high and bring to a boil. Remove from heat and stir in the queso cheese and the cheddar cheese.

5. In a bowl, combine the cornmeal, flour, and baking powder. Slowly add the butter, eggs, orange juice, honey, buttermilk, sour cream, and salt. Mix until well blended.

6. Add the cornmeal mixture to the top of the skillet and spread evenly around.

7. Place the skillet in the oven and bake for 20 minutes, or until cornmeal crust is golden brown and firm.

Serves: 4

Preparation time: 10 minutes

Cooking time: 15 minutes

Ingredients:

- 2 teaspoons olive oil

- 6 cups bok choy, cut into chunks

- 2 tablespoons butter

- 16-20 sea scallops

- 4 cloves garlic crushed and minced

- 1 tablespoon jalapeno pepper, diced

- ½ cup of sugar

- ¼ cup of rice vinegar

- ½ cup of water

- 1 teaspoon salt

- 1 teaspoon black pepper

Preparation:

1. Prepare a 10 or 12-inch cast iron skillet and heat the olive oil over medium heat. Add the bok choy and sauté until crisp-tender, approximately 4-5 minutes. Remove from the pan and set aside. Keep warm.

2. Add the butter to the skillet and melt over medium heat. Add the scallops, garlic and jalapeno pepper. Cook the scallops 1-2 minutes per side, while lightly tossing the other ingredients.

3. Add the sugar, rice vinegar, and water to the skillet. Stir well and let cook for 3-4 minutes, allowing flavors to blend.

4. Serve scallops and sauce over sautéed bok choy.

Italian Beef and Tomatoes

Serves: 4

Preparation time: 10 minutes

Cooking time: 25 minutes

Ingredients:

- 2 pounds choice beef steak, approximately 1½ inch in thickness

- ¼ cup olive oil, divided

- 5 cloves garlic, crushed and minced

- 4 cups mini tomatoes of various colors, halved

- 3 cups fresh spinach, torn

- 1 sprig fresh rosemary

- 1 tablespoon fresh thyme

- ½ cup fresh basil, chopped

- 1 teaspoon of sea salt

- 1 teaspoon ground black peppercorns

- 3 tablespoons olive oil, divided

Preparation:

1. Preheat oven to 375°F/191°C.

2. Prepare a 12-inch cast iron skillet and heat two tablespoons of the olive oil over medium-high heat.

3. Add the garlic and sauté for 1 minute. Add the tomatoes and sauté for 2 minutes before adding the spinach. Cook for an additional 1-2 minutes, or until spinach is lightly wilted. Remove contents with a slotted spoon and set aside.

4. Add the remaining oil to the skillet. Once the oil is hot, add the steaks and season with salt and ground black peppercorns. Sear the steaks on each side, until brown, approximately 7 minutes per side.

5. Add the tomatoes and spinach back into the pan. Season with rosemary, thyme, and basil. Place the skillet into the oven and bake until steak reaches desired doneness, approximately 6-10 minutes.

6. Let rest 10 minutes before serving.

Italian Sausage Baked Spaghetti

Serves: 4

Preparation time: 10 minutes

Cooking time: 30 minutes

Ingredients:

- 1 pound ground Italian sausage

- 1 tablespoon vegetable oil

- 4 cloves garlic, crushed and minced

- 1 cup yellow onion, diced

- 1 28-ounce can crushed tomatoes, with liquid

- ¼ cup fresh parsley, chopped

- ½ cup fresh basil, chopped

- 1 tablespoon fresh oregano, chopped

- 1 teaspoon salt

- 1 teaspoon black pepper

- 2 cups chicken stock or water

- ½ pound spaghetti noodles

- ½ cup fresh mozzarella pearls

- ½ cup parmesan cheese, freshly grated

Preparation:

1. Preheat oven to 400°F/204°C

2. Prepare a 12-inch cast iron skillet and heat the vegetable oil over medium-high heat. Add the Italian sausage to the pan and cook until browned, approximately 5-7 minutes. Drain any excess grease from the skillet.

3. Add the garlic and yellow onion. Sauté for 2-3 minutes, or until onions are tender.

4. Add the tomatoes, with liquid, and season with parsley, basil, oregano, salt, and black pepper. Stir well

5. Add the chicken stock or water and bring to a low boil. Add the pasta to the pan, pushing it in to make sure that the sauce covers the noodles. Cook for 10-12 minutes, or until pasta is al dente.

6. Mix in mozzarella and parmesan cheeses. Place skillet into the oven and bake for 15-20 minutes.

Creamy Green Vegetable Skillet Pasta

Serves: 4

Preparation time: 10 minutes

Cooking time: 15 minutes

Ingredients:

- ¼ cup butter

- 2 cloves garlic, crushed and minced

- ¼ cup scallions, sliced

- 2 cups broccoli florets

- 2 cups zucchini, sliced

- 2 cups spinach, torn

- ½ teaspoon crushed red pepper flakes

- 1 teaspoon salt

- 1 teaspoon black pepper

- 1 cup vegetable stock

- ½ cup heavy cream

- ½ cup cream cheese softened

- ½ cup parmesan cheese, freshly grated

- ¼ cup fresh basil, chopped

- ½ cup fresh parsley, chopped

- 1 tablespoon fresh chives, chopped

- 1 pound bow tie pasta, cooked

- Lemon zest for garnish, if desired

Preparation:

1. Prepare a 12-inch cast iron skillet and heat the butter over medium heat. Add the garlic and scallions, cook for 1 minute.

2. Add the broccoli and zucchini. Sauté for 2-3 minutes. Add the spinach to the skillet and sauté for 1-2 additional minutes. Season with crushed red pepper, salt, and black pepper.

3. Remove the vegetable mixture from the skillet and set aside.

4. To the skillet, add the vegetable stock over medium-high heat and bring almost to a boil. Reduce heat to medium. Slowly stir in the heavy cream and add the

cream cheese, stirring the entire time, until a smooth consistency is achieved.

5. Reduce heat to low and add the parmesan cheese, basil, parsley, and chives. Mix well.

6. Add the vegetables and pasta back to the pan and toss well to mix. Let simmer for 3-4 minutes, or until warmed through.

7. Serve garnished with lemon zest, if desired.

Beef and Rosemary Dumplings

Serves: 6

Preparation time: 15 minutes

Cooking time: 35 minutes

Ingredients:

- 2 pounds beef stew meat

- ¼ cup flour

- 1 teaspoon paprika

- 1 teaspoon garlic powder

- 1 teaspoon black pepper

- 1 teaspoon thyme

- 2 tablespoons butter

- 2 cloves garlic, crushed and minced

- 1 cup red onion, chopped

- ½ cup celery, diced

- 2 cups beef stock

- 1 cup apple cider

- 1 cup carrots, chopped

- 1 cup fresh peas

- 1 cup parsnips, chopped

- ¼ cup flour

- ¼ cup seasoned bread crumbs

- 2 tablespoons vegetable shortening

- 1 tablespoon fresh rosemary, chopped

- 1 teaspoon fresh dill, chopped

- ½ teaspoon salt

- ½ teaspoon black pepper

- 1 egg, beaten

Preparation:

1. In a bowl combine ¼ cup flour, paprika, garlic powder, black pepper, and thyme. Toss the stew meat pieces into the seasoned flour to coat. Set aside.

2. Prepare a 12-inch cast iron skillet and heat the butter over medium heat. Add the garlic, red onion, and celery. Sauté for 2-3 minutes.

3. Add the beef and cook until browned, approximately 5 minutes.

4. Add the beef stock and apple cider, scraping the pan. Increase the heat to medium-high and bring to a boil.

5. Reduce heat to medium-low and add the carrots, peas, and parsnips. Cover and simmer for approximately 45 minutes.

6. While stew is cooking, combine ¼ cup flour, bread crumbs, vegetable shortening, rosemary, dill, salt, black pepper, and egg. Mix until a dough forms. Using tablespoon sized mounds, form the dough into rough ball-shaped dumplings.

7. Place the dumplings in the stew and cook an additional 15 minutes before serving.

Deep Dish Beef Lovers Pizza

Serves: 4-6

Preparation time: 15 minutes

Cooking time: 30 minutes

Ingredients:

- 1 pound flank steak, sliced into thin strips

- 2 cloves garlic, crushed and minced

- ¼ cup shallots, sliced

- 2 cups portabella mushrooms, sliced

- 1 teaspoon crushed red pepper flakes

- 1 teaspoon salt

- 1 teaspoon black pepper

- 2 tablespoons olive oil, divided

- 1 ball premade pizza dough, enough for one large pizza

- 1 cup canned fire roasted tomatoes, drained

- 1 cup heirloom tomatoes, sliced

- ½ cup smoked Gouda, cut into very small cubes

- 1 cup fresh mozzarella, shredded

- ½ cup parmesan, freshly grated

Preparation:

1. Preheat oven to 425°F/218°C.

2. Prepare a 12-inch cast iron skillet and heat 1 tablespoon of the olive oil over medium heat.

3. Add the steak strips, garlic, and shallots. Cook, stirring, for approximately 5 minutes, or until steak has almost reached desired doneness. Add the mushrooms, red pepper flakes, salt, and black pepper and sauté an additional 2 minutes.

4. Using a slotted spoon, remove the contents and set aside. Let skillet cool enough to be handled.

5. Roll out the dough into a large circle at least 14 inches in diameter. Press the dough directly into the pan, on top of any pan drippings that remained. Spread the dough along the bottom of the skillet and up along the sides.

6. Brush the dough with the remaining olive oil and add a layer of the heirloom tomatoes. Next add the beef and mushroom mixture, followed by the Gouda cheese.

7. Add the fire roasted tomatoes and spread them as evenly over the top as possible. Top with mozzarella and then parmesan cheese.

8. Place the skillet over medium heat and cook for 3-5 minutes before placing in the oven and baking 15-20 minutes or until crust is golden brown and cheese is bubbly.

9. Let rest slightly before serving.

All in One Hamburger Casserole

Serves: 4

Preparation time: 10 minutes

Cooking time: 20 minutes

Ingredients:

- 1 pound ground beef

- 1 cup red onion, diced

- 2 cups tomatoes, diced

- ¼ cup ketchup

- ¼ cup yellow mustard

- ¼ Worcestershire sauce

- ¼ cup dill pickles, diced

- 1 tablespoon vegetable oil

- 4 cups shredded potatoes, moisture removed

- 1 teaspoon garlic powder

- 1 teaspoon oregano

- 1 teaspoon salt

- 1 teaspoon black pepper

- 1 cup cheddar cheese, shredded

Preparation:

1. Prepare a 12-inch skillet and add the ground beef over medium heat. Cook until lightly browned, 4-5 minutes. Drain any fat.

2. Add the red onion and tomatoes. Cook for 3-4 minutes. Season with ketchup, yellow mustard, Worcestershire sauce, and dill pickles. Mix well. Remove from the skillet and set aside.

3. Add the vegetable oil to the pan and increase heat to medium-high. Add the shredded potatoes. Cook, while tossing, for 3 minutes. Season with garlic powder, oregano, salt, and black pepper. Press the potatoes into the pan and cook for 5 minutes, or until the bottom becomes crispy.

4. Add the ground beef back into the skillet and toss with the potatoes. Cook for an additional 3-5 minutes, or until heated through.

5. Top with shredded cheddar cheese before serving.

Chapter 7: Desserts

Lemon Poppy seed Dump Cake

Serves: 8

Preparation Time: 5 minutes.

Cooking time: 30 minutes

Ingredients:

- 1 package lemon pudding mix

- 1 package Golden Cake mix

- ¼ cup poppy seeds

- 1 ½ cup milk

- ½ cup white chocolate chips

- 6 ounces butter, melted

Topping ingredients

- 3 tablespoons poppy seeds for topping

Preparation:

1. Preheat oven to 350 degrees, lightly coats a cast iron large skillet with a little butter.

2. In a bowl, combine lemon pudding mix, poppy seeds, Golden cake mix, milk, Golden Cake mix, and butter, mix well

3. Pour batter into cast iron skillet, sprinkle with poppy seeds for topping.

4. Bake cake in the oven for 30 minutes.

Cinnamon Raisin Nut Dump Cake

Serves: 8

Preparation Time: 5 minutes.

Cooking time: 20 minutes

Ingredients:

- 1 package Spice Cake mix

- 2 cups of milk

- ½ cup raisins

- ¼ cup walnuts

- ½ teaspoon cinnamon

- Butter

Preparation:

1. Preheat oven to 350 degrees and coat cast iron large skillet with a little butter.

2. Mix remaining ingredients in a bowl, and pour into a large cast iron skillet. Place in the oven for 20 minutes.

Serves: 6

Preparation time: 10 minutes

Cooking time: 10 minutes

Ingredients:

- 4 eggs

- 4 cups of milk

- 1 teaspoon vanilla bean, crushed

- ½ cup maple syrup

- ½ teaspoon salt

- Butter

Preparation:

1. Whisk eggs in a bowl, mix in vanilla, maple syrup, and salt.

2. Pour milk into cast iron pot, bring to simmer.

3. Remove milk from the stove.

4. Add a tablespoon at a time of hot milk into the egg mixture, mixing continuously in order not to cook an egg.

5. Once the egg mixture has been tempered with milk, whisk egg mixture into the pot of milk.

6. Return pot to stove, and simmer for 5 minutes.

7. Cool and serve.

Raspberry White Chocolate Dump Cake

Serves: 8

Preparation time: 5 minutes.

Cooking time: 35 minutes

Ingredients:

- 1 package raspberry pudding mix

- 1 package Angel Food Cake mix

- 1 ½ cup milk

- ½ cup white chocolate chips

- 6 ounces butter, melted

Preparation:

1. Preheat oven to 350 degrees, lightly coats a cast iron large skillet with a little butter.

2. In a bowl, combine milk, raspberry pudding mix, Angel Food Cake mix, and white chocolate chips.

3. Pour batter into cast iron skillet, drizzle with butter, and place in the oven for 35 minutes.

Apple Caramel Cake

Serves: 8

Preparation Time: 15 minutes.

Cooking time: 25 minutes

Ingredients:

- 2 medium-sized Gala apples, peeled, cored

- ½ cup walnuts

- ½ cup caramel candies

- 1 cup all-purpose flour

- ½ cup brown sugar

- 3 eggs

- 2 teaspoons baking powder

- ½ teaspoon vanilla

- ½ teaspoon ground cinnamon

- ¼ teaspoon ground cloves

- ¼ teaspoon salt

- Coconut oil

Preparation:

1. Preheat oven to 350 degrees, coat a 10" cast iron skillet with a little coconut oil

2. Thinly-slice half an apple for topping, dice remaining apple.

3. Place 1/3 cup coconut oil and brown sugar in a food processor, mix.

4. Add eggs to butter mixture and beat.

5. Sift flour and combine with cinnamon, cloves, salt, and baking powder.

6. Slowly add dry ingredients to a food processor, continue mixing.

7. Add vanilla, walnuts, caramel candies, mix.

8. Pour mixture into cast iron skillet, top with apple slices and place in the oven for 25 minutes.

Serves: 12

Preparation time: 15 minutes

Cooking time: 25 minutes

Ingredients:

- 3 cups almond flour

- 2 teaspoons flax meal

- 2 eggs

- 2 tablespoons water

- ½ teaspoon salt

- Almond oil

Filling ingredients

- Fresh berries, peaches

- Whipped Cream

Preparation:

1. Whisk eggs, and gradually add in almond flour, mix.

2. Add 1 teaspoon almond oil, salt, flax meal, water, and continue mixing until smooth.

103

3. Heat 2 tablespoons almond oil in 10" cast iron skillet, spoon 3 tablespoons mixture into skillet.

4. Cook for a minute per side.

5. Stuff with fruits and whipped cream, serve.

Serves: 6

Preparation time: 15 minutes

Cooking time: 35 minutes

Ingredients:

- 5 Granny Smith apples, peeled, cored, diced

- ½ cup walnuts, crushed

- ½ cup brown sugar

- ¾ cup all-purpose flour

- ½ cup rolled oats

- 1 teaspoon cinnamon

- 1 cup butter

Topping ingredients (optional)

- Vanilla Ice Cream

Preparation:

1. Preheat oven to 350 degrees.

2. Place ¼ cup butter in cast iron deep skillet, melt over medium heat.

3. Add apples, walnuts, and ½ teaspoon cinnamon to skillet,

4. Continue to stir until apples are soft and 80 percent of water has dissipated approximately 12 minutes.

5. In a separate bowl, combine brown sugar, flour, rolled oats, ½ teaspoon cinnamon and remaining butter.

6. Crumble mixture with a fork.

7. Sprinkle crumbs over apples, and stick into oven for 20 minutes.

8. Serve with creamy vanilla ice cream.

Conclusion

Cast iron cookware makes whipping up a full three-course meal a snap, even during weekdays. The recipes provided in this book give you a chance to sample a variety of dishes from the traditional to those with ethnic influences. The diversity also gives you a chance to check out the numerous ways you can use cast iron in the kitchen.

If you've had a chance to try out the dishes, we hope you enjoyed them and are inspired to whip up a few of your own as well. If you have yet to start creating, then rest assured you are in for a treat of the fabulous taste sensation kind.

We hope this meal collection will bring you ease of cooking and provide you with more time to spend with your family - that's what it's all about.

Made in the USA
Monee, IL
02 December 2019